Zen and the Art of Piracy

Geoffrey Wilkinson

Copyright © Geoffrey Wilkinson 2024

Geoffrey Wilkinson has asserted his right under the Copyright, Designs and Patents Act 1988 to be identified as the author of this work. All rights reserved. No part of this publication may be reproduced, stored in a retrieval system, or transmitted in any form or by any means, electronic, mechanical, photocopy, recording or otherwise, without prior written permission of the copyright owner. Nor may it be circulated in any form of binding or cover other than that in which it is published and without a similar condition including this condition being imposed on a subsequent purchaser.

A CIP catalogue record for this book is available from the British Library.

ISBN 978-1-9160622-2-1

Published by Geoffrey M. Wilkinson
Franksbridge
Llandrindod Wells
Powys LD1 5SA
United Kingdom

for Susan and Bryn

Acknowledgements

My thanks to John Krummel for his suggestion, in personal correspondence, that it is best to discuss the Buddhist notion of emptiness (*śūnyatā*) in relation to dependent arising (*pratītyasamutpāda*). This essay began as my attempt to do so.

The illustrations on pages 20 and 22, which come from the sequence of *Ten Oxherding Pictures* attributed to Shūbun, are reproduced by kind permission of the Jōtenkaku Museum in the precincts of the Shōkokuji Temple, Kyōto.

Zen and the Art of Piracy

Many, many years ago I spent a summer in Kyōto, Japan. Mornings were taken up with study at a language school. In the afternoons I was free to explore a good number of the cultural treasures, especially temples and gardens, in and around the city. One day I visited the Jizō-in, a small Zen temple in a particularly tranquil setting among groves of bamboo near Arashiyama. I was probably there an hour or two. As I was leaving I stopped at a small book stall and bought a set of reproduction woodblock prints, accompanied by a booklet in Japanese and English. The English-language text was attributed to Suzuki Daisetsu, the scholar of Buddhism better known in the West as D.T. Suzuki.[1] Oddly, though, it was full of misprints and other typographical errors. Since the errors do not occur in Suzuki's book, we have to suspect a sloppy and unauthorized reprint, possibly in breach of copyright. At the time I assumed it had been produced by the temple itself, which conjured up the delightfully incongruous image of devout monks engaged, wittingly or unwittingly, in an act of literary piracy. Disappointingly, I have since discovered that the same booklet was on sale at other Zen temples, which suggests the piracy had a common (and maybe less devout) origin elsewhere.

But what of the content? What is the Suzuki text about?

The answer is nothing. Or rather, nothingness. Or *emptiness*.

Seven varieties of emptiness

To the best of my understanding, the most fundamental single principle of Mahāyāna Buddhism is that there is no such thing as *ātman*. In its Buddhist (as opposed to Hindu) sense, this Sanskrit word is synonymous with *svabhāva*, which is sometimes translated as 'self' or

---

[1] The text, as originally published in Suzuki's *Manual of Zen Buddhism*, can be found in my References under Suzuki (1935), pp. 150-71. I explain a bit more about it on p. 17 below.

'essence', now more often as 'inherent existence'.[2] Mahāyāna metaphysics begins with the refutation of *ātman* (its doctrine of *nairātmya*) and the refutation of *svabhāva* (*niḥsvabhāva*)[3] — that is, with the denial of inherent existence. Moreover, it is a denial that extends not just to individual human beings, as terms such as 'self' might suggest, but to everything in the universe, animate and inanimate, sentient or otherwise.[4]

To say that something has no inherent existence is to say that, lacking ontological independence, it does not exist in its own right and that, by definition, it is mutable and impermanent. For if it is devoid of 'essence' or 'self-nature', there is nothing 'in' it to remain fixed and unchanging for eternity: it will come to be according to causes and conditions that are not (for want of a better phrase) of its own making, and will cease to be once those causes and conditions cease to apply.

Now while Buddhists may deny that there is such a thing as *ātman*, they do not deny that there is such a thing as a table, for example. So we are entitled to ask how come a table is a table if, by their reckoning, it does not exist in its own right. In reply I cannot hope to improve on the following commentary by Jay Garfield, a scholar and translator specializing in Tibetan Buddhism. By his account, to say that a table has no inherent existence (or, as Tibetans would put it, that it does not exist 'from its own side') is to say that 'its existence *as the object that it is — as a table*' depends on its relations both with other things in the world and with ourselves. Its reality is not inherent or independent, it is conventional:

> That is, if our culture had not evolved this manner of furniture, what appears to us to be an obviously unitary object might instead be correctly described as five

---

[2] Other English translations include 'self-nature', 'self-substance', 'own-being', and even 'soul'. In Chinese canonical translations of the Sanskrit, *ātman* is rendered as 我 [literally, 'self'] and *svabhāva* as 自性 ['self-nature']. For these and other Chinese terms I have consulted the glossary at the back of Suzuki (1930).

[3] Again the Chinese is pithily expressive: 無我 ['non-self'] for *nairātmya* and 無自性 ['lacking self-nature'] for *niḥsvabhāva*.

[4] The denial of inherent existence in human beings is known as *pudgalanairātmya* in Sanskrit; 人無我 ['person non-self'] in Chinese. Apropos 'true' self (what is left once we are rid of the perception that we exist inherently as an 'I' or 'me' or ego self), see pp. 18-21 of my main text.

objects: four quite useful sticks absurdly surmounted by a pointless slab of stick-wood waiting to be carved. Or we would have no reason to indicate this particular temporary arrangement of this matter as an object at all, as opposed to a brief intersection of the histories of some trees. It is also to say that the table depends for its existence on its parts, on its causes, on its material, and so forth. Apart from these, there is no table.[5]

Lest we assume, mistakenly, that a table only exists in this sense because it is a man-made object, Garfield emphasizes that the same can be said of any natural object, including a tree:

> The boundaries of the tree, both spatial and temporal (consider the junctures between root and soil, or leaf and air; between live and dead wood; between seed, shoot, and tree); its identity over time (each year it sheds its leaves and grows new ones; some limbs break; new limbs grow); its existence as a unitary object, as opposed to a collection of cells; etc., all are conventional.[6]

The principle that everything relies on something else for its conventional existence has a name: *pratītyasamutpāda* in Sanskrit,[7] variously translated as 'relational origination', 'dependent origination', 'dependent arising' and 'dependent co-arising'. For consistency with most of the translations I have come across, I stick with dependent arising. That it follows (arises?) from the denial of inherent existence (i.e., from the doctrine of *niḥsvabhāva*) is very characteristic of Mahāyāna metaphysics, which describes reality in terms that are often so closely interrelated as to be interchangeable or synonymous.

---

[5] Garfield (1995), pp. 89-90. His italics. There is an interesting (and possibly misleading) comparison to be made here with Heidegger's door handles and hammers as examples of 'equipment [*Zeug*]' that may be 'ready-to-hand [*zuhanden*]' or 'un-ready-to-hand [*unzuhanden*]' in relation to some 'for-the-sake-of-which [*Worum-willen*]' acceptable to 'the "they" [*das Man*]', i.e., conventionally acceptable. Passages in which these Heidegger terms occur in context can be found by referring to the glossary and/or indexes in Heidegger (1927).

[6] Garfield (1995), footnote 6 on p. 90. In turn, Garfield credits Graham Parkes for this observation.

[7] 綠起 ['relational arising'] in Chinese.

Another such term is *advaya*, which translates as 'non-dualism' or 'non-duality'.[8] One way of approaching *advaya* — and I warn that the following is a personal interpretation which may or may not be correct doctrinally — is to see it as an unavoidable consequence of Mahāyāna's refutation of any attempt to define reality positively. The definitions are always negative. There is no *ātman*, no 'essence', no 'self-nature', nor inherent existence by any other name. And yet, as represented by our table, things do exist.[9] In other words, Mahāyāna seems to be implying that there are two distinct realities: the familiar and conventional sort, which is mere appearance or illusion and therefore a reality in name only; and something else, something we do not experience conventionally, which is more 'real' and qualifies as 'true' or 'ultimate' existence. Surely, we object, Mahāyāna confronts itself with a contradiction, a circle that cannot be squared. How can there be two realities? To which a Buddhist would respond, I think, that there is indeed a circle but not one in need of squaring. For although it is true to say that no thing exists inherently, it is also true to say that even a thing lacking in inherent existence does not fail to exist at all or, if you'll forgive the awkward expression, does not *non-exist*. The fact of its having no inherent existence and the fact of its conventional existence are not mutually exclusive. They are complementary, one and the same reality. There is no duality of an existence and a non-existence. Already we have an inkling of where Mahāyāna Buddhism is taking us with its insistence on defining reality by negatives: the full significance of *advaya* will soon be clearer.

Yet another core term or principle, and the one to which the discussion so far has been leading, is *śūnyatā*.[10] It is helpful to start with the etymology of the Sanskrit word, which, as I understand, is an abstract noun derived from an adjective, *śūnya*, meaning 'empty' — hence 'emptiness' (or 'nothingness') for *śūnyatā*. The root word may be *śvi*, which conveys the idea 'to swell' and makes for the subtle image of something swollen on the outside (such as a gourd or a balloon) but

---

[8] 無二 or 不二 [literally, 'not two'].

[9] Or as Garfield would say, the table represents 'the empirical reality of things': Garfield (1995), p. 102.

[10] *Śūnyatā* is translated into Chinese as 空 [literally, 'empty', 'emptiness' or 'void']. One of several synonyms is *anutpāda* [不生], which Suzuki translates as 'no-birth' or 'unborn' and discusses in relation to the *Laṅkāvatāra Sūtra*: Suzuki (1930), especially pp. 239-40 and 287-92.

hollow or empty inside. Hold on to that image because it offers an intuitive way into the meaning of *śūnyatā*, which can be completely baffling if we first try to grasp it through reason and logic.

The image works as a metaphor for conventional existence: if the external appearance of the swollen object stands for the undeniable existence of things in the world, its hollowness reminds us that they are conventional and have no inherent existence of their own. They are empty.

To some extent the same metaphor works for the principle of *advaya*, non-duality, but not well enough to avert all risk of bafflement because the emptiness implied by *advaya* defies, and even affronts, the kind of reason and logic that we recognize. Which is to say, it implies *the emptiness of everything in the universe*. Right. We need to retrace our steps. To say that a thing has no inherent existence sounds like saying that it does not exist at all. As we now know, however, that is not what Buddhism professes: on the contrary, it professes that a thing's lack of inherent existence does not preclude its conventional existence because they are one reality, not two. To maintain this position, it would seem, Buddhism has to make a choice or 'take sides', giving priority to one over the other: either the 'true' and 'ultimate' reality is that no thing exists, albeit it appears to exist; or the 'true' and 'ultimate' reality is that things do exist, albeit it sounds as if they do not. To put it another way, Buddhism seems faced with a choice between nihilism (ultimately no thing exists) and something akin to 'eternalism' (ultimately things exist).[11] Which is it? Buddhism's escape clause, so to speak, is that in the great emptiness of the universe it is not meaningful to conceive of non-existence as having priority over existence, or vice versa. They are empty concepts in an empty universe.

In the English-language literature and doubtless elsewhere, Buddhists and scholars of Buddhism, including D.T. Suzuki and his successors in Japan, humour our demand for 'reasonable' and 'logical' explanations of reality by characterizing *śūnyatā* as dynamic and dialectic. Yes, they concede, on the face of it there is a mutual contradiction between non-existence or 無 ['non-being', pronounced *mu* in Japanese] and existence or 有 ['being', *u* in Japanese]. But by refuting nihilism, which negates 'eternalism', *and* refuting 'eternalism',

---

[11] By 'eternalism' I mean the position that a thing exists because it manifests an immutable and eternal 'essence' or 'substance'; 'akin to' because of course Buddhism itself denies the very notion of 'essence' or 'substance'.

which negates nihilism, *śūnyatā* achieves (again for want of a better expression) a double negation. The result, according to Buddhism, is an affirmation — seemingly paradoxical yet an absolute affirmation — of everything that is in the universe just as it is, here and now, and in all its variety and fullness. Personally I am wary of any attempt to explain *śūnyatā* 'logically' because it encourages us to go on thinking in exactly the terms that Buddhism warns against: dualistic terms, renamed 'non-being' and 'being' or 無 and 有, but dualistic nonetheless. Difficult as it may be, I suggest that intuition remains the better guide to *śūnyatā*.[12] And intuition tells us, I think, that we have arrived at the profoundest principle of Mahāyāna Buddhism: *the emptiness of everything in the universe is synonymous with its just-as-it-is-ness, its immediacy, distinctiveness, and repleteness*. The Sanskrit name for this principle is *tathatā*, which translates into English as the very appropriate if little used word 'suchness'.[13] About which I have more to say later.

According to the *Laṅkāvatāra Sūtra*, a text thought to date from about the fourth century AD and important for an understanding of Zen and other Buddhist schools, there are seven types of *śūnyatā*.[14] That is more emptinesses than are manageable, so I shall pick out only two of them. The first is *svabhāva-śūnyatā*, the 'emptiness of self-substance', which is of crucial significance but need not detain us long because we have already met it under a slightly different name: *niḥsvabhāva* (the doctrine that there is no such thing as 'essence' or 'self-nature': my page 2 above).[15] The second of my two types of *śūnyatā* deserves more attention because it takes us to an aspect of Mahāyāna metaphysics that we have not yet encountered (or not knowingly). This is *lakshaṇa-*

---

[12] A Zen Buddhist would say, I imagine, that disciplined meditation and related practices are the best guide.

[13] Also sometimes translated as 'thusness'; 眞如 [literally, 'true like-ness' or 'true as-ness'] in Chinese.

[14] The *Laṅkāvatāra Sūtra* count is actually quite conservative. According to the doctrine of *aṣṭādaśa-śūnyatā* [十八空名], there are eighteen types of emptiness.

[15] The interchangeability of the two terms is particularly clear in Chinese: *svabhāva-śūnyatā* is rendered as 自性空 ['self-nature void'], compared with 無自性 ['lacking self-nature'] for *niḥsvabhāva*.

śūnyatā, the 'emptiness of appearance',[16] which the *Laṅkāvatāra Sūtra* describes as follows:

> Existence is characterized by mutual dependence; individuality and generality are empty when one is regarded apart from the other…. [T]here are, after all, no aspects of individuation such as 'this', 'that', or 'both'; there are no ultimate, irreducible marks of differentiation. For this reason, it is said that self-appearance is empty.[17]

The *Laṅkāvatāra Sūtra* alludes here to the anomaly that we experience the world in dualistic terms — 'this/that', 'subject/object', 'me/not-me', and so on — despite the fact Buddhism insists that reality knows no dualities. The sūtra's explanation for the anomaly is *vikalpa*, 'false discrimination',[18] which leads us to divide up or *particularize* the world and perceive differentiations in it where none exist. As the sūtra puts it more explicitly,

> [we] are attached to a variety of external objects; [we] go from one form of discrimination to another, such as the duality of being and non-being, oneness and otherness, bothness and not-bothness, permanence and impermanence, … etc.[19]

Consistently with Mahāyāna doctrine, the first line of the first passage above maintains that the world we see around us comes from dependent arising, the mutual dependence of one thing upon another: fundamentally our world and the larger universe are empty. And yet elsewhere the sūtra seems to speak of reality as *citta* or 'Mind' and, even more emphatically, *cittamātra* or 'Mind-only'.[20] By this the sūtra does not mean, however, that the emptiness of the universe is a product of the human mind (which would make *cittamātra* an extreme and odd

---

[16] 相空 ['aspect void' or 'devoid of aspect'].

[17] From the translation by D.T. Suzuki in Suzuki (1930), p. 288.

[18] In Chinese 分別 ['discrimination', here understood as 'false discrimination']. *Vikalpa* relates to *vishaya* [境界], which is translated as 'the principle of particularization' in Suzuki (1930), p. 174.

[19] Suzuki (1930), p. 246.

[20] In Chinese *citta* is rendered as 心 [literally, 'heart' meaning 'mind'], *cittamātra* as 唯心 ['exclusively heart/mind'].

form of idealism), only that *the world as we experience it* is a product of the mind. *Cittamātra* is a sort of rhetorical device without which it would be impossible even to attempt to communicate the reality of emptiness — beyond conventional language and therefore inexpressible — to the unenlightened ('the ignorant', as the *Laṅkāvatāra Sūtra* terms them), for whom conventional language is the only currency of communication.

The effect of *vikalpa* is that Mind itself is differentiated into eight aspects, the eight *vijñānas*,[21] five of sense-perception and three that we might loosely and variously call consciousness, intellect, cognition, and the like. While these doctrinal complexities are somewhat obscure, happily the sūtra also characterizes *vikalpa* and its effects by means of a simple metaphor. Mind is likened to an ocean, tranquil and perfectly calm — calm, that is, in the sense of being absolutely free of discrimination or duality of any kind. In other words, in its original state Mind is synonymous with emptiness. But the ocean is ruffled by the 'wind of individuation', which disturbs the perfect calm and sets waves dancing.[22] The 'wind of individuation' is *vikalpa*, the false working of Mind; the dancing waves are 'this' and 'that', 'subject' and 'object', 'me' and 'not-me', and the countless other dualities that *vikalpa* brings into the world.

Nāgārjuna

Among Mahāyāna Buddhists the most authoritative and revered of philosophers is Nāgārjuna, who probably lived in southern India some time between 150 and 250 AD. The work for which he is best known, still studied to this day, is the *Mūlamadhyamakakārikā* or *Treatise on the Middle Way*.[23] In particular, he is credited with clearly articulating the principle of *śūnyatā*, which, though implicit in the doctrine of

---

[21] The eight *vijñānas* [八識] are discussed in the context of the Mind-only doctrine, and in great detail, in Suzuki (1930), pp. 169-99. One of the eight *vijñānas* (and, confusingly, a synonym for *citta*) is *ālaya* [藏], which has the literal meaning of 'storehouse': some of the connotations are explained on Suzuki's pp. 176-77.

[22] The ocean/waves metaphor recurs in the verse *gāthās* translated on pp. 171-73 of Suzuki (1930).

[23] In the Garfield translation, on which I mostly rely, the title is rendered as *The Fundamental Wisdom of the Middle Way*.

dependent arising as taught by the Buddha, was not explicitly developed before Nāgārjuna's time. I am not qualified to judge the merits of that claim, but it is hard to read his famous treatise without concluding that he is largely responsible for the Mahāyāna practice of refuting everything and defining reality by negatives. For evidence we need look no further than his opening verses, dedicated to the Buddha, which include four pairs of negations (also known as the eight or eightfold negations):

> Whatever is dependently arisen is
> Unceasing, unborn,
> Unannihilated, not permanent,
> Not coming, not going,
> Without distinction, without identity,
> And free from conceptual construction.[24]

My understanding of these lines is as follows. If something is dependently arisen, by definition it is empty and lacks inherent existence. Nāgārjuna means it is 'unborn', therefore, in the figurative sense that there is nothing to be 'born' in the first place and, by the same token, that there is nothing to 'cease' either — which is why 'unborn' is paired with 'unceasing'.[25] Likewise, although something dependently arisen is mutable and impermanent (because it has no 'essence' or 'self-nature' capable of remaining fixed for eternity: page 2 above), it does exist conventionally — hence the 'not permanent/unannihilated' pairing. By 'Not coming, not going,' I take Nāgārjuna to mean that while can we speak of things coming to be and ceasing to be in the conventional sense (according to causes and conditions prevailing at the time: pages 2-3), *fundamentally* it is meaningless to think of anything as having an existence that 'comes' or 'goes'. 'Without distinction, without identity' means that, lacking inherent existence, things are neither the same as each other nor different (whereas if they did exist inherently, sameness and difference would be the only relations possible between them). The last line, 'And free from conceptual construction', is nicely ironic at its own expense:

---

[24] Dedicatory Verses as translated in Garfield (1995), p. 100.

[25] I assume, I hope correctly, that the Tibetan word Garfield translates as 'unborn' has the same nuance as the Sanskrit word (*anutpāda*) in the *Laṅkāvatāra Sūtra* which Suzuki translates as 'no-birth' or 'unborn', i.e., that Garfield's 'unborn' is also a synonym for 'empty/emptiness': my footnote 10.

reality is ultimately beyond conceptual thought and yet here we are, it is saying, only able to express our eightfold negations because we have conceptualized reality in terms of contrasting pairs (i.e., false dualities).[26]

Nāgārjuna's dedicatory verses are not just some florid embellishment. Far from it. They announce the central theme of the whole treatise and define the Middle Way of its title: the eightfold negations *are* the central theme and they are the Middle Way.[27] We'll come back to the definition of 'Middle Way'. For now let's stay with the eightfold negations and how they determine the content of Nāgārjuna's treatise.

To recap, according to Mahāyāna Buddhism reality is *śūnyatā* or emptiness, which is synonymous with *tathatā* or suchness (the immediacy and just-as-it-is-ness of things: page 6). *Śūnyatā-tathatā* cannot be attained so long as we are obstructed or distracted by dualities of any kind. Conversely, *sunyata-tathatā* is what is left, so to speak, when all dualities are denied. Thus the eightfold negations determine Nāgārjuna's content in the sense that, right at the outset, they categorically deny every conceivable duality (birth/extinction, impermanence/existence, 'coming/going', sameness/difference) to open the way towards emptiness and suchness. And that way takes the form of a systematic exposition (which at times anticipates and answers the objections of imagined interlocutors) of what we are left with when we arrive at reality just as it is.

As there are many divergent interpretations of Nāgārjuna's treatise, I shall focus on only a small number of passages that are not, I believe, the subject of major controversy. The first is verse 38 of Chapter XXIV:

XXIV.38   If there is essence, the whole world
           Will be unarising, unceasing,
           And static. The entire phenomenal world
           Would be immutable.[28]

---

[26] Or to put it another way, and borrowing an image from Garfield, the last line of the Dedicatory Verses forewarns of the 'logical tightrope act' that Nāgārjuna has to sustain 'at the very limits of language and metaphysics': Garfield (1995), p. 102.

[27] As succinctly expressed in the Chinese: 八不中道 [literally, 'eight-negations-middle-path' or, more elegantly, something like 'Middle Way of the Eightfold Negations'].

[28] Garfield (1995), p. 317.

Nāgārjuna often argues by asking what the world — the 'phenomenal world' — would be like if things existed not just conventionally but inherently. The answer here is that it would be *static and incapable of change*. Why? Because for something to exist inherently it would need to have an 'essence' or 'self-nature', yet for its 'essence' or 'self-nature' to change would make a nonsense of its supposed inherent existence. In turn, and remembering that Buddhism is a religion of salvation, this passage is saying implicitly what Nāgārjuna says more explicitly elsewhere:[29] that such a world would leave no scope for meaningful human effort towards salvation, for what would be the point of trying to escape suffering in a world of eternal and immutable 'essences' and 'self-natures'?

Of all the many verses that have to be read multiple times before their meaning registers, the following is almost in a class of its own:

XIII.7   If there were anything not empty,
         Then something empty would also exist.
         If there is not anything not empty,
         How could the empty exist?[30]

Only when we have negotiated the convoluted syntax do we realize what the verse is saying: if anything other than emptiness existed inherently, then so would emptiness; but as in fact no thing exists inherently, nor does emptiness. In other words, even the existence of emptiness is conventional, not inherent, because *emptiness is itself empty*. If you are flummoxed by the notion of the emptiness of emptiness (*śūnyatā-śūnyatā*), think for a moment of the alternative if emptiness did exist inherently. Emptiness would be the essence to end all essences, the 'essence of emptiness' that somehow lay behind and supported the conventional existence of the universe and everything in it. Yet in reality there is no such essence, as we can demonstrate by considering once more our humble example of conventional existence, the table (pages 2-3). Lacking inherent existence, the table is empty. If we try to analyze its emptiness, though, what do we find? 'Nothing at all,' replies Garfield in his commentary,

---

[29] Especially in the very next verse, XXIV.39, and verses 24-25 earlier in the same chapter: Garfield (1995), pp. 317 and 309-10.

[30] Napper (1989), p. 130. Napper's translation is also from the Tibetan. For comparison, Garfield's translation is on his p. 211.

but *the table's* lack of inherent existence. No conventional table, no emptiness of the table. The emptiness is dependent upon the table and is, therefore, itself empty of inherent existence, as is the emptiness of *that* emptiness, and so on, ad infinitum.... Emptiness is hence not different from conventional reality — it is the fact that conventional reality is conventional. Hence it must be dependently arisen since it depends upon the existence of empty phenomena. Hence emptiness itself is empty.[31]

However much we may think we have adjusted to the vocabulary of Mahāyāna metaphysics, in which key principles and terms are so freely interchanged, it is still dizzying to be told that emptiness is no more and no less than the conventional character of conventional existence. It is as if we have passed a point of no return — the point at which we finally grasp that the universe has absolutely no grounding whatsoever, not even in an essence of its own emptiness.

There is much more that could and should be said about the content of Nāgārjuna's treatise. It is high time, however, that we returned to the definition of the 'Middle Way' of its title, which takes us to verse 18 of Chapter XXIV. While still treading carefully around detailed issues of doctrine, I will venture to quote two subtly different translations, representing two subtly different interpretations, of the verse. Here is the first:

XXIV.18 Whatever arises dependently
We explain as emptiness.
That [emptiness] is itself a dependent designation
And it is the Middle Way.[32]

The import of the first two lines is clear enough: dependent arising and emptiness are two aspects of one and the same reality. The subtlety is in line three: in this translation, which is partly based on a commentary by the fourteenth-century Tibetan philosopher Tsongkhapa, the otherwise ambiguous determiner 'That' is identified explicitly with

---

[31] Garfield (1995), p. 316. His italics.

[32] Adapted from the translation in Napper (1989), pp. 185 and 755. As I understand Napper's note 352, '[emptiness]' in her translation indicates a gloss by Tsongkhapa in his commentary *Ocean of Reasoning, Explanation of* [Nāgārjuna's] *'Treatise on the Middle Way'*.

'emptiness'. Besides reiterating that emptiness itself is empty ('is itself a dependent designation'), the effect is to define emptiness as the Middle Way (or the Middle Way as emptiness, depending how we care to express it). So far, so good. But perhaps it is not the whole story, as the second translation suggests:

XXIV.18   Whatever arises dependently
We explain as emptiness.
That, being a dependent designation,
Is itself the Middle Way.[33]

In version two, which also happens to be via Tibetan and not directly from Nāgārjuna's Sanskrit, the ambiguity of 'That' is left as it is. Once again the effect is to stress the emptiness of emptiness, yet now the definition of 'Middle Way' is significantly broader and more complex: the Middle Way has to be understood, we are told, not only as emptiness, but as emptiness, dependent arising, *the relation between the two* and, for good measure, the verbal conventions that allow us to talk of a Middle Way at all. Personally speaking, and lacking any knowledge of Tibetan (or Sanskrit), I can't help feeling that the second translation rings truer than the first. In any case, either translation brings us back to the same reality: the interchangeability of dependent arising, conventional existence and emptiness, which is reiterated in Nāgārjuna's next verse:

XXIV.19   Because there is no thing
That is not dependently arisen,
There is no thing
That is not empty.[34]

The phrase 'Middle Way' connotes, of course, a middle path between extremes and this nuance is also there in Nāgārjuna's title. After all, his whole treatise steers a very delicate path between the extremes of nihilism and 'eternalism' (pages 5-6). That is why verse 10 of Chapter XV, in particular, reads as it does:

---

[33] Adapted from the translation in Garfield (1995), p. 304. In his Introduction to the Commentary, pp. 97-98, Garfield explains that his reading of Nāgārjuna is heavily but not exclusively influenced by the Gelukpa tradition of Tibetan Buddhism, established primarily by followers of Tsongkhapa.

[34] Adapted from Napper's translation: Napper (1989), pp. 185-86.

XV.10 To say 'it is' is to grasp for permanence.
To say 'it is not' is to adopt the view of nihilism.
Therefore a wise person
Does not say 'exists' or 'does not exist'.[35]

The Ten Oxherding Pictures

I began with one act of piracy, of unknown attribution, and it is time for another, unapologetically my own. My piracy consists in appropriating Buddhism to answer a question that Buddhism itself does not ask, or does not ask directly: how do we accommodate ourselves to our current knowledge, based on robust scientific evidence, of the origins of the universe? Our knowledge, that is, that the world and we ourselves *literally* come from nothing. For we now understand that we are made of the same stuff as the universe, matter that happened to burst into being at an arbitrary instant 13.8 billion years ago, out of nothing and without reason, necessity or purpose.

Buddhism does not ask this question of our current knowledge because, as it seems to me, it has no interest in the universe of matter and energy studied by science. (Nor is it interested in the universe in terms of a divine creation story, because for Buddhists the idea of a creator God implies a false duality of creation and creator: on a related issue, more anon.) Nonetheless, and speaking as a non-Buddhist, I would say that Mahāyāna Buddhism offers us unfamiliar but profound language and imagery to express the reality of the world we find ourselves in. While we may balk at the Buddhist notion that the universe is empty, is that notion any more outlandish or disturbing than the evidence, presented to us by physics and cosmology over the past century, that the first constituents of the universe just popped into existence out of a great nothingness? And we don't have to subscribe to the doctrine of dependent arising to recognize that in a nominal sense, at least, everything in the world is indeed connected with and dependent upon something else — the table that is only 'a table' in relation to its constituent parts and the uses to which we put it, the tree that is only 'a tree' in relation to its evolutionary ancestors and the botanical classification we choose to apply to it, and so on, and so on. Profoundest of all is Buddhism's insistence that there is no contradiction between a world that comes from nothing (from the

---

[35] Garfield (1995), p. 224.

emptiness of *śūnyatā*) and the undeniable existence of the world as it is and as we experience it (the conventional world). In other words, and contrary to common misperceptions of Mahāyāna metaphysics, to say that the world has no inherent existence is not to say that it has no existence at all, or that it exists in some separate and inferior realm of reality. For Buddhism there is only one reality and it encompasses both absolute nothingness and absolute somethingness — or maybe we should call it *everythingness*, the conventional existence of every possibility of being, inanimate and animate, that has come or might ever come from the nothingness. True, says Buddhism, the universe is empty in that no thing in it exists inherently. But the conventional world is inconceivably *full*, replete with every possibility of existence that dependent arising can bring into being.

You may object that Buddhism gets from nothingness to everythingness only in a metaphysical or metaphorical sense, whereas physics and cosmology get there on the theoretical and observational evidence of the Big Bang and chemical evolution. The language of science is and should be definitive in accounting for the literal origins of the universe. It is less well suited, I think, to conveying the quality that Buddhism calls the suchness of things, the reality that each existence is uniquely just as it is and could not be such, *could not be at all*, unless it had originated in nothing. In Mahāyāna terms, the explanation for this has to do with the doctrine of the emptiness of emptiness (*śūnyatā-śūnyatā*). That is, if emptiness were *not* empty, it would have an 'essence' (the 'essence of emptiness': page 11) and that is all there would be — or rather, not be — because an eternal and immutable 'essence of emptiness' would not permit the existence of anything of any kind, let alone anything unique in its suchness.

My own interpretation is more idiosyncratic, not doctrinal, for I take suchness as confirmation — albeit still in a metaphysical or metaphorical sense — that the universe and its contents are not the work of a creator, and particularly not one conceived of anthropomorphically as a personal Being. To make a universe, it strikes me, a creator would at least have a motive or impulse to act, more likely a purpose or plan. Which means that from the very start each and every existence, each and every possibility of being, would be constrained by the need to conform with the motive or purpose. Even if the universe is the work of a creator, therefore, it might have been a different universe, not the one we know, if the creator's motive or purpose had been different. Yet it would futile to speculate on how it might have been different because it is unknowable: all we can say is that some existences would have been possible, others not, but we cannot say what or precisely why. My point is that no individual existence would have the leeway, so to speak, or freedom to be just as it is because its being would always be determined by the creator's motive or purpose, whatever that happened to be. And what if, on a whim, the creator had decided not to make a universe after all? By a different route, we appear to come to the same conclusion as Buddhist metaphysics: no world of independent existences, but now no just-as-it-isness either.

Paradoxical as it may seem to us, only an absolute nothingness — the very antithesis of a creator Being — can give rise to the suchness of anything and everything.

The language of science is especially poor at conveying the human dimension of suchness — the reality that we, too, are uniquely just as we are and that it is our condition not to be otherwise. Of all the possibilities of being that have emerged from the nothingness, it is *our* possibilities and *our* suchness that have come to be. It is not, as it might sound, a condition we are only capable of realizing in some sort of exalted or mystical state: if only we knew it, it is evident in the very ordinariness of our daily lives. Particularly in the context of an essay on Zen Buddhism, I can think of no better (or earthier) way of expressing this than to quote the ninth-century Chan master Linji, who stressed that Buddhism does not require any special effort: 'You have only to be ordinary,' he said, 'defaecating, urinating, dressing, eating, and lying down to rest.'[36] I can't see that we have to be doctrinal Buddhists to appreciate Linji's teaching as a striking affirmation of the extraordinariness — the suchness — of the ordinary. And not just an affirmation, but an implicit injunction to be aware of our suchness at every moment of our lives. Linji is not inviting complacency, egoism, idleness, fatalism, or any other attitude to life. Our suchness is what we start with, not an end in itself, and it does not explain (or excuse) what we go on to do (or not do) with our lives. But he does invite us to consider that, precisely because the ordinary moments of our lives are so unremarkable and

---

[36] Adapted from Ruth Sasaki's translation of Discourse XII in the *Linji lu*, a collection of sayings attributed to Linji: Sasaki (2009), pp. 11-12 and 185. In the original Chinese this passage begins 祇是平常無事, which translates literally as 'just be ordinary, nothing to be done'. In Japan Linji is known as Rinzai, and the school of Buddhism associated with him as Rinzai Zen.

even trivial, we should pay all the more attention to them and recognize the suchness in them.[37]

My answer to my own question — how do we accommodate ourselves to the fact that we literally come from nothing? — is, then, that we should adopt and celebrate the Buddhist notion of suchness. For although Buddhism itself may seem to dismiss the mundane and conventional world as a worthless illusion, the reality (and, as I understand, Nāgārjuna's view) is that our world, the mundane and conventional world, is *not* an empty illusion. It is full, replete with every possibility of being, and fully valid in its own right — validated by the just-as-it-isness of everything and everyone that is, has been and might ever be.

I also said earlier that Mahāyāna Buddhism offers us profound, if unfamiliar, language and imagery to express the reality of our world. Well, hopefully the language of suchness — virtually interchangeable with emptiness and dependent arising — is somewhat more familiar by now. As for the imagery, I need to explain about the prints that I bought at the Jizō-in all those years ago, and how they relate to the Suzuki text that came with them. Reproduced from woodblocks by the twentieth-century Japanese artist Tokuriki Tomikichirō, the prints comprise a sequence of images known as *The Ten Oxherding Pictures*. The pictures, which originated within the Chan tradition of Buddhism in China and are equally valued among Zen Buddhists in Japan, are essentially a visual device to aid practitioners of Chan or Zen at various stages of their journey towards enlightenment. The best known version of *The Ten Oxherding Pictures* is associated with the twelfth-century Chan priest Kuoan, whose verses in Chinese are often included in other versions of the pictures. Suzuki's text, simply titled 'The Ten Oxherding Pictures', is one of at least two translations he made of Kuoan's verses.[38]

---

[37] Elsewhere, and in the context of a discussion of the twentieth-century Japanese philosopher Nishida Kitarō, I have suggested that we have a *moral* responsibility to acknowledge our suchness, and that this may be what Nishida meant when he said, 'The laws of morality ... come to be included in the laws of reality': Wilkinson (2024), p. 103. The Nishida quote comes from the book for which he is probably best known, *An Inquiry into the Good*: Nishida (1911), p. 126.

[38] The translations that follow in this essay are my own. Suzuki's original text was illustrated with plates of the series of *Ten Oxherding Pictures* attributed to a fifteenth-century painter, Tenshō Shūbun, closely associated with the Shōkokuji, a Zen temple

As their title suggests, the pictures depict an ox and its herder, who is sometimes represented as a young boy. The herder first stands for what we experience as our individual self, the 'I/me' or ego self, busily and perhaps contentedly engaged in the everyday affairs of the conventional world and yet vaguely aware that it is not 'true' self and that the conventional world alone is not the whole of reality. The ox stands for 'true' self, which, empty of inherent existence, is synonymous with the emptiness of the universe. One indication of the complex dynamic at work in the sequence is that the herder appears in only eight of the ten pictures, and the ox in only four.

For a reason that will soon be clear, I'm going to jump straight to Picture Ten, which is titled 'Nonchalantly Entering the Marketplace'.[39] In the Tokuriki print, it depicts the herder as an amiable if dishevelled old man, bare-chested, a staff in one hand and an empty gourd (an image for *śūnyatā*) in the other. He is conversing with a small boy, maybe his younger self, and their meeting symbolizes the relation between the enlightened old man (who now stands for 'true' self), other people, and the world in general. For the point is that the old man is *in* the world, not secluded away somewhere in the guise of a holy hermit. And the world he has returned to (or rather, never left) is the *conventional* world, so conventional, indeed, that it might have come straight from one of Linji's discourses: the world of the marketplace, peopled not just by butchers (particularly bad Buddhists because they kill living creatures) and other tradespeople but all manner of fallible human beings, carousing, swilling and doing everything else that fallible humans do. It helps to know that in his bare-chested and grubby state the old man takes on the guise of the Chan monk Pu-tai (known as Hotei in Japan), a jolly, pot-bellied figure beloved of children. In turn, Pu-tai is said to be a manifestation of the Bodhisattva Maitreya (Miroku Bosatsu in Japan), who is moved by the compassionate wish to help all sentient beings achieve enlightenment. Of the many commentaries on Picture Ten, I think the simplest and best is by the Japanese philosopher (and lay practitioner of Zen) Ueda Shizuteru:

---

in Kyōto. For copyright reasons, my illustrations are also from the Shūbun scroll (ink and light colours on paper), which remains in the keeping of the Shōkokuji.

[39] The title, 入鄽垂手, has been variously translated. I take 垂手 to mean 'with arms loosely by his sides', suggesting carefreeness or nonchalance. ('Slouching into the Marketplace' is tempting but may be overdoing the nuance!)

> One's own awakening to the true self is confirmed in bringing others to awakening in such a way that it is their own awakening…. What we have here [in Picture Ten] is the transmission of the self, from self to self. [40]

Or yet another way of putting it is to say that Picture Ten is the beginning rather than the end of the sequence.

The titles of Pictures One to Six are relatively straightforward. In order, and literally translated, they are: 'Searching for the Ox'; 'Finding Traces of the Ox'; 'Finding the Ox'; 'Catching the Ox'; 'Taming the Ox'; and 'Returning Home on the Ox's Back'.[41] Suffice to say that these titles characterize the first six of the stages in which the relation between the herder (the 'I/me' self) and the ox ('true' self) changes and gets progressively closer. The title of Picture Seven is 'The Ox Forgotten, the Person Remains'.[42] Not so straightforward, it signals a critical stage: the herder appears to have attained 'true' self (seemingly symbolized by the image of him sitting alone, the ox nowhere to be seen) but only appears to have done so. The nuance behind 'the Person Remains' is that, despite all the progress he has made, the herder is still in danger of falling back into 'I/me' selfhood: which is to say, again in the words of Ueda Shizuteru, 'fall[ing] back into … a self-consciousness that reckons "I am now what I should be" — which is [Ueda stresses] but a sublimer form of religious egoism'.[43] So long as the least residue of self-consciousness remains, the herder may still perceive himself as a subject (an 'I/me' or 'person') in pursuit of an object ('true' self).[44]

And so we come to Pictures Eight and Nine, which I think are qualitatively different from the others and, within the limited scope of this essay, merit fuller treatment.

---

[40] Ueda (1982), pp. 21-22. Ueda, acknowledged as the central figure of the third generation of the so-called Kyōto School of philosophy, died in 2019.

[41] In the original Chinese: 尋牛; 見跡; 見牛; 得牛; 牧牛; and 騎牛歸家.

[42] 忘牛存人.

[43] Ueda (1982), p. 13.

[44] An alternative way of interpreting the sequence from Picture One to Picture Seven is, I suppose, as a working out of the doctrine of *pudgalanairātmya* (the denial of inherent existence in human beings: my footnote 4).

Picture Eight. Ox and Person Both Forgotten
人牛俱忘

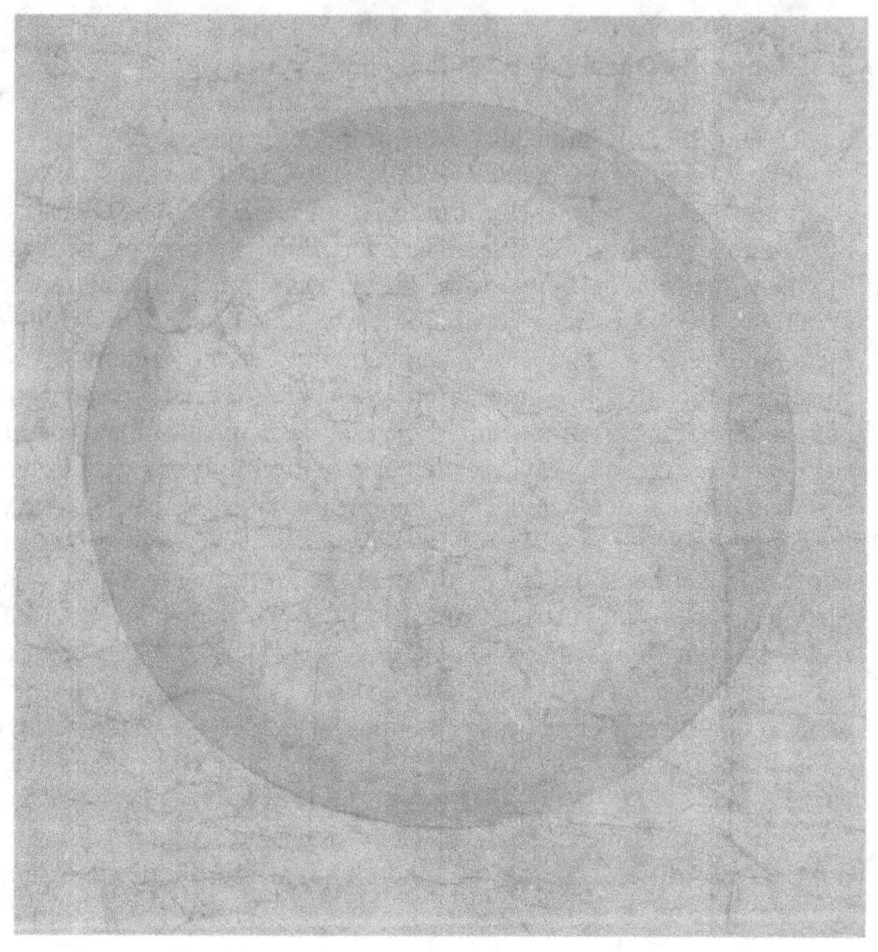

Whip, halter, herdsman and ox — all empty.
No words convey the vastness of the sky.
There is no place for a snowflake on a red-hot furnace.
Now in true accord with [the teaching of] the patriarchs.

I interpret Kuoan's verses under Picture Eight (in my own translation) as follows:

> Whip and halter stand for the emptiness of all inanimate things in the conventional world; the herdsman now for the emptiness of 'true' self (i.e., *selfless* self, rid of 'I/me' or 'person'); the ox more explicitly for emptiness (*śūnyatā*) itself and, by implication, the emptiness of emptiness (*śūnyatā-śūnyatā*). The emptiness (as the sky) is not susceptible of expression in conventional language, and the emptiness (the red-hot furnace) leaves no 'place' for false discrimination (*vikalpa*, the snowflake). The last line reminds us that the *Ten Oxherding Pictures* are primarily for the benefit of serious practitioners of Chan/Zen, who deserve recognition for attaining this momentous stage in their journey (and who, implicitly, are also warned against dwelling on their attainment as if it were an end in itself).

Now for the piracy. Appropriating the language and imagery of *śūnyatā* (inseparable from *tathatā*, suchness), I propose, offers the prospect of an accommodation with our scientifically-based knowledge of how the universe began. An *intuitive* accommodation, I mean, not explicable logically or even rationally but, informed as it is by two thousand years of Buddhist reflection on the nature of reality, not to be dismissed as incoherent metaphysics or mysticism. The appropriation involves taking a few liberties with Kuoan's verses and reinterpreting them:

> Protons, neutrons, stars, galaxies, our world, we ourselves — all came from nothing. Unintelligible it may be, yet the universe is under no obligation to make sense to us and it is pointless to look for design, purpose, reason or necessity in its origins. Grasp that and we grasp intuitively what the patriarchs of physics and cosmology have been trying to tell us for the past one hundred years or more.[45]

---

[15] The patriarchs I mean here include not just Edwin Hubble (who in 1929 provided the first observational evidence that the universe is expanding) but Georges Lemaître, the Catholic priest who both recognized that an expanding universe must have had a *beginning* and came remarkably close to anticipating the Big Bang theory. Invoking quantum physics, Lemaître wrote: 'If we go back in the course of time we must find fewer and fewer quanta [of energy], until we find all the energy of the universe packed in a few or even in a unique quantum': Lemaître (1931).

Picture Nine. Returning to the Source
返本還源

So much striving to return to the origin, return to the source.
Far better to have been blind and deaf from the outset.
Sitting alone in the serenity of his hut, he sees no thing outside.
The river flows on just as it is; the flower is red just as it is.

'So much striving', says Kuoan, all that effort, only to find what has been true and should have been clear from the beginning: the 'I/me' self seeking enlightenment (the herdsman) and the supposed object of the seeking (the ox) are one and the same reality. 'Far better to have been blind and deaf': blindness = seeing without a seer, deafness = hearing without a hearer, i.e., 'far better' = without a seeing or hearing subject as opposed to a seen or heard object. The hut symbolizes the absolute serenity of the 'true', empty self — no subject within the hut and no object outside. 'The river flows....' is a beautifully simple evocation of suchness, the just-as-it-is-ness, immediacy, distinctiveness, and repleteness of the reality represented by the flowing river and the red flower.[46] Emptiness-suchness is the origin, the source. No trace of anything else remains, not even Buddhism or the Buddha.

The language of science, I have suggested, is well suited to explaining how our universe literally came out of nothing; not so well suited to expressing the suchness of everything that exists. The language and imagery of Buddhism — Mahāyāna metaphysics in particular — make a better job of that, which is why I have appropriated the *Ten Oxherding Pictures* in the way I have. On reflection, however, it is hard to escape the strange redundancy encapsulated in Kuoan's 'So much striving': namely, while it appears enlightenment cannot be attained without going through the stages set out in the *Ten Oxherding Pictures*, with enlightenment comes the realization that the stages were never really necessary in the first place. In a sense, therefore, to go on interpreting and reinterpreting Kuoan's verses would only compound the striving by saying more when too much has been said already. Instead, I end with another question: if the *Ten Oxherding Pictures* are a roundabout expression of suchness, what does a direct expression look like? Is there a single image that would take us straight to the heart of suchness — not as a *there* (Picture Nine)

---

[46] My translation of the fourth line of Kuoan's verse, which in the Chinese reads 水自茫茫花自紅, borrows from the 1969 translation by M.H. Trevor quoted in Ueda (1982), p. 15: 'Boundlessly flows the river, just as it flows. Red blooms the flower, just as it blooms.' As I take Ueda to suggest on p. 17 of his commentary, the character 自 evokes 自然, meaning literally 'to be as it is by itself' or, more specifically here, the suchness (or thusness: footnote 13) of the river and flower.

to be arrived at step-by-step, stage-by-stage, but as a spontaneous intuition that everything has been *here* all along, just as it is and not otherwise.

My personal choice for a single image, a poetic image rather than a woodblock print, is a haiku by the eighteenth-century Japanese poet Yosa Buson. Given the pervasive influence of Buddhism in Japanese culture, it is not unreasonable to speculate that Buson himself might have meant the haiku as an expression of suchness.[47] As I can offer no firm evidence either way, however, I must caution that my reading of the haiku may constitute yet another instance of piracy. In for a penny, in for a pound, let me rephrase my question: if the *Ten Oxherding Pictures* were a Buson haiku, which one would it be? My answer, suchness in seventeen syllables, would be…

---

[47] It may or may not be significant that for a time Buson was a lay priest in the Jōdo or Pure Land sect (which, like Zen, is classed as part of the Mahāyāna tradition, albeit Jōdo is very different indeed from Zen in doctrine and practice). The haiku I have chosen comes from a collection published in 1784, one year after Buson's death. The translation is my own.

白露や茨の刺にひとつづゝ
shira-tsuyu ya
ibara no hari ni
hitotsu zutsu

glistening dew —
on the briar's thorns
each a single drop

References

Garfield, Jay (1995). *The Fundamental Wisdom of the Middle Way* (New York: Oxford University Press, 1995). English translation of the Tibetan text of Nāgārjuna's Sanskrit *Mūlamadhyamakakārikā*.

Heidegger, Martin (1927). *Being and Time*. Translation of *Sein und Zeit* by John Macquarrie and Edward Robinson (Oxford: Blackwell, 2003).

Lemaître, Georges (1931). 'The Beginning of the World from the Point of View of Quantum Theory' in *Nature* Vol. 127, No. 3210 (9 May 1931), p. 706.

Napper, Elizabeth (1989). *Dependent-Arising and Emptiness* (Boston, MA: Wisdom Publications, 1989). The scope of Napper's book is indicated by her subtitle: *A Tibetan Buddhist Interpretation of Mādhyamika Philosophy* [the Middle Way philosophy of Nāgārjuna] *Emphasizing the Compatibility of Emptiness and Conventional Phenomena*.

Nishida, Kitarō (1911). *An Inquiry into the Good* (New Haven: Yale University Press, 1990). Nishida's first major work, *Zen no kenkyū*, translated by M. Abe and C. Ives.

Sasaki, Ruth, translator (2009). *The Record of Linji* (Honolulu: University of Hawai'i Press, 2009). Translation of the *Linji lu*, sayings of the Chan priest Linji, also known as Rinzai in the Japanese pronunciation of his name. Edited by Thomas Kirchner. Includes the Chinese text.

Suzuki, D.T. (1930). *Studies in the Laṅkāvatāra Sūtra* (London: Routledge/Eastern Buddhist Society, 1930). By a strange coincidence, my edition (New Delhi: Motilal Banarsidass Publishers, 1999) is semi-pirated: bought new in Wales although clearly marked FOR SALE IN SOUTH ASIA ONLY.

—— **(1935).** 'The Ten Oxherding Pictures' in his *Manual of Zen Buddhism* (Kyōto: Eastern Buddhist Society, 1935), pp. 150-71. Second edition (1950) published in London by Rider & Co. and reprinted several times since.

Ueda, Shizuteru (1982). 'Emptiness and Fullness: Śūnyatā in Mahāyāna Buddhism' in *The Eastern Buddhist* Vol. 15, No. 1 (Spring 1982), pp. 9-37. Translated by James Heisig and Frederick Greiner.

Wilkinson, Geoffrey (2024). *Regaining to Know Aright: 'Natural' Knowledge for a Secular World* (Franksbridge, Powys: Geoffrey M. Wilkinson, 2024).

www.ingramcontent.com/pod-product-compliance
Lightning Source LLC
Chambersburg PA
CBHW071128130526
44590CB00056B/2984